INTRODUCTION

You are on your way

Dear reader,

First, congratulations on getting this far. This means you are interested in growing your business and willing to take action.

This attitude is not for everyone, but it is vital because the world changes at an ever faster pace. People who stop evaluating their work and looking for ways to improve are often left behind.

The world is being transformed by technology in particular. Unlike the past, which saw many local retailers, logistics technology has allowed for the creation of large superstores. Information technology advances enabled a lot more sales to be moved onto the internet. Both of these developments favor the large corporations, creating a winner-takes-all situation. Amazon's business plan is to take small retailers out business.

Here are some more examples. Ten years ago, many small taxi companies existed. Today, apps like Uber are commonplace and smaller businesses are closing. Advertising was distributed across multiple publications and outlets fifteen years ago. Today, advertising is dominated by Google and other internet giants. Technology and economies of scale are making it difficult for smaller businesses to survive.

This has not happened in the hotel business, thanks to the popularity of small hotels and the level playing field provided by online travel agents. However, this does not mean that things aren't changing. In many ways, they get more difficult. It is dangerous to ignore these changes and risk becoming a victim.

What is the impact of change on the hotel industry?

My hotel selections for my gap year were governed by Lonely Planet reference to the hotel. Today, I don't think it is possible to take one person's outdated opinion.

You wouldn't even think about. You know that the reviews system has made a significant impact on the hotel industry. Those who are able to use it to their advantage greatly benefit.

I was limited to the Lonely Planet Guide's small selection of hotels. Today, I can view almost all hotels, big and small, via my smartphone. This is great news for small hotels, but how do you stand out? How can you make your hotel stand out among the rest?

Since Basil Fawlty's days, when he would place an expensive advertisement in a prestigious magazine to attract a higher class of customer, the entire process of attracting customers and then generating repeat business has changed tremendously.

Online travel agents have more influence than tour operators. The industry's democratization offers higher rewards for those who are most knowledgeable about the new system.

Understanding the new order

This book is about how to understand this new system. Not all hotel owners know how to use the system in a specific way.

You will most likely already know some of these tips or have used them yourself. You will be doing a great job keeping up to date with industry developments if you have all the tips. It will be worthwhile even if you don't know all of them. A reminder of key concepts and a push towards greater implementation will make it a productive hour of reading.

This book is concise and offers practical tips that will help you improve your business. I don't want you to waste your time but I want to help your company. The average reader will find it takes around an hour to read. It focuses on quality and not quantity. It is small enough to carry in your pocket or bag, and large enough for notes. You could not ask for more. The book can be accessed in sections if you want to see a more detailed discussion of certain points.

These are

1-How to best use online travel agents

2—Pricing

3-Selling on Value and Not Price

How to improve your 4-Review scores

5--Your website and all other selling channels

6—Other Business Improvements

I hope that you find this book useful. You can explore many of the ideas in this book and find more if they interest you. You may also like to download the business checklist I provide at www.roompricegenie.com/checklist. This checklist will help you identify areas that could be improved in your hotel. It might be a good idea to have this book with you, so you can fill it out as you read the book.

About me

Ari Andricopoulos is my name. My father and his partner run a bed and breakfast on the Isle of Wight. I manage a software company that helps smaller hotels to manage their revenue, RoomPriceGenie. You can find it at www.roompricegenie.com - where you can also sign up for an email giving more advice and discussion on how to improve your business. Software that will help you accomplish a few of these objectives is also available.

THE TIPS

Here's a meta-tip before we get into the tips section. A good property management system is essential to ensure your hotel runs at its best. You can use a spreadsheet or your own database to manage your hotel's bookings, but you should move to a commercial management software system as soon as possible.

Why? Because technology is increasingly important and commercial property management systems were designed to be flexible with it. You will reap the benefits sooner if you make this difficult switch sooner than you think.

Can your system send the same rooms to Booking.com Expedia Hotels.com and your site? Is it able to automatically adjust the number available rooms when you sell one? Your system cannot automatically adjust the number of rooms available when you sell one. This is a sign that your system is not maximizing the potential of online travel agents. This means that you are making more administrative work and exposing yourself to more mistakes.

It's better to act now and do the difficult transition than wait. Even if you choose the wrong system, it's easier to transfer all your data to another system once it is established. It is the installation of the first system that is most difficult.

Beds24 is a flexible, economical and excellent system that I recommend. It costs around 20 EUR per month and increases as you add rooms or channels. However, it offers all the services that your hotel requires and doesn't limit you in any way like other systems. The only problem is that they are relatively inexpensive and the customer support is mostly online. It is also important to remember that it is flexible and can take some getting used to. However, it is worth it in end.

We are also able to recommend other products with different price tags. Please call our office for more information. They can be more user-friendly and offer better customer service. They can make assumptions about your company that could be restrictive.

You will need to have a reservation system in order to look at other systems.

1--A channel manager that connects via API to online travel agents.

2--A booking engine that connects with your website to make direct bookings. These bookings automatically go into your system.

3--Make sure they have an API that allows you to take out information and add it in. Many do not, which can limit your ability to use third-party applications.

4--Check that you can easily change prices on an evening basis, rather than seasonal. Some systems assume you only change prices once a year.

If you need assistance with this change, contact us at www.roompricegenie.com and we can help you to migrate your system.

SECTION CH6

ONLINE TRAVEL AGENTS

Online travel agents (OTAs), are websites such as Booking.com and Hotels.com that bring together a variety of hotels to make it easier for guests to compare and select options. These websites will be used by many people and you will be familiar with their importance.

This is a prime example of how technology can be used to eliminate smaller players. It takes a lot more expertise to survive as a travel agent today, in order to be able compete with the variety and value offered by websites such as Booking.com.

The OTAs can be expensive. They charge 20-25% of your income (in some cases, income including VAT). A rate parity clause states that you cannot offer your room for less on your own website. Despite the restrictions and high costs, these OTAs offer a great service for hotel owners - if they fully take advantage.

OTAs have two major advantages:'reach and the billboard effect'. Reach means you can reach new customers that you wouldn't otherwise be able to attract. This means that you're increasing your revenue even if you were already fully booked.

The OTAs provide great exposure and advertising for your hotel. This is known as the 'billboard effect'. Potential clients are seeing you and may prefer to book directly through your website, even if they have seen you via an online travel agent. They know that they may be able to get better deals if they book directly and might also want to support smaller hotels. You can also turn a guest who has booked through Expedia into a repeat client by allowing them to book through your website in the future.

How can you make the most of online travel agents' opportunities?

1--GET HIGHER ON THE PAGE.

Website visitors are lazy. 75% of the traffic to Expedia's results page goes to the first 15 hotels. These are the people you want to be. But how can you get there?

You can pay more to be a top choice. This is a way to test if the increased bookings are worth the extra expense. You will pay 5% more but it may be worth it if you get 20% more bookings than you have and aren't full anyway.

You don't have to pay anything extra to climb higher. How can an online travel agency make the most revenue? They will list the most desirable hotels first in their listings. Your profile will attract more bookings if it has quality content (see below for more information) They will also get more bookings if you offer a competitive price.

However, OTAs take a long-term perspective. They want their websites to have as many bookings as possible from hotels. They will place you higher if you provide them with more capacity. If you're not busy, offer all of your rooms.

2—HIGH QUALITY CONTENT

Online travel agents are constantly testing what sells. Because they have so many data, they are able to make a good guess about which hotels are most appealing. Would you like to find out what hotels sell the best? Photos. Photos. There are many of them. Professionally-taken photos are well worth the cost. I highly recommend it.

People want to see everything. Photos of the rooms, bathrooms, common areas, and the garden. Everyone loves to eat, so make sure you take nice photos of it.

Did you know that 60% travelers consider bathroom images very important? Take photos of your bathrooms.

Great photos are more important as you become more expensive. While budget hotels may offer basic features, higher-end luxury hotels will require lots of photos. You want your hotel to be a quality establishment, no matter its size?

Let me repeat: The more photos you have, and the better they are, the more rooms that you can sell.

3—CLEAR, FACTUAL TEXT

People want to know what they're getting. Tests by OTAs have shown that hotel rooms are sold more when they contain detailed, accurate text. Flowery language doesn't. You can get a copywriter for the job if you are able. It should be sales-oriented and list the benefits for guests. The text should also be written in simple language.

4--LISTEN TO ALL YOUR BENEFITS AND AMENITIES.

Hotel owners make the mistake of not listing all the hotel's benefits. These benefits are not obvious. Take a look at the reviews. If guests like your location, they might say that they love it and consider it the best in the region. Give details about what guests can do in the area. If guests like the garden, describe how popular it is.

It is really a shame to miss out on amenities. Mention that you have good and free wifi. Mention that you have ironing facilities. Mention if there is a safe in your room. People will book rooms with more amenities.

5—MANAGE OTA AVAILABILITY

This is the basic rule: If you are not fully booked, give as much availability to online agents as possible. However, limit your availability when OTAs take over direct sales.

As we have already mentioned, OTAs will reward you for making them available. You can also sell more if you give more. It is worth selling all the rooms if you know that your room will not be booked.

You may also want to limit supply in busy seasons to ensure that you can sell most of your rooms to customers directly over the phone or via your website.

My opinion is that price is the best way to manage room demand. I recommend raising the price if things are so crowded that you will be booked full even with OTAs.

This exception would only apply when there is a lot of demand, such as for local concerts. Because you don't want your loyal guests to leave, you shouldn't charge too much. Instead, you can control the demand through other methods. One could be adding a minimum stay requirement while another might only sell directly. Both will give you more income and lower the price. More information will follow.

It is important to understand that if your pricing is correct, you don't need to leave any room for the OTAs.

6--HOW MANY OTAS SHOULD YOUR HOTEL BE SOLD THROUGH?

Maintaining your presence on multiple OTAs takes more effort, as you probably know. It is important to create your profile and keep it updated on any changes. Your reservation system should make it easy to use any number of channels on a daily basis.

As we have already mentioned, being on OTAs will give you extra exposure and the benefit from the billboard effect. Your rooms will be seen more often if you have more OTAs. As many OTAs as you can support, I recommend. If you don't get any bookings from one, you can cut them off. This will help you find the ones that work best for you.

7--WHEN DO AVAILABILITY OPEN?

It is a good idea to plan your rooms at least 12 months ahead of time. There are two reasons for this. As mentioned, the first is that the more you are available on the OTAs, the better your results will be. The second is much simpler. You won't be able to book if you're not there. It doesn't hurt to be available for bookings, even if there are only a few reservations made over 11 months.

8—RESPOND TO REVIEWS

Remember how I mentioned that online travel agencies had stats for every aspect of their business? They do. Another thing they discovered was that hotels who respond to negative reviews get more bookings. The caveat is that you must respond positively to negative reviews. Accept criticisms and list what you intend to do differently. You don't need to be defensive or attack the guest.

These reviews are read by people who feel the guest is better taken care of and that negative reviews have less impact.

SECTION TWO

PRICING

It is vital to get your pricing correct. RoomPriceGenie.com is my company. It was specifically created to address the problems that smaller hotels face in this region.

Imagine having 10% more income. Profit is almost always possible in the hotel industry because of its high fixed costs. What would you do? In winter, you could keep the doors closed for longer. You can do whatever refurbishments you wish. You could take nicer vacations.

Although it sounds like a quick way to get rich, this is the truth. You are losing out if you don't adjust your prices to meet demand every day. You can do 10% more with the resources that you have if you learn how to change pricing.

This is why? When making holiday plans, most people choose the location first and then the hotel. This ensures that your area has a fixed number of visitors. But where do they go to stay?

The price of a product can make a huge difference in your decision. Value is a key factor. The best value room is the one that meets their requirements. A hotel's ability to offer a discount is one way to determine its value. Hotels that have their prices changed are displayed on the OTAs as offering a discounted rate. Take a look at this offer:

Woodlands Luxury Spa PS150 PS75

This hotel is better than any other listed at PS75, but without the strikethrough?

Your hotel's value is the sum of the price and the benefits you offer. This determines how likely they are to book it. The less likely they will book with your competitor, the better.

It is difficult to find hotels in a competitive market. There must be losers in order to have winners.

This is what the larger hotels realize and hire revenue managers at PS30,000 per year. To get the right price, they use expensive software.

But you can do the same at a tiny fraction of the cost - see www.roompricegenie.com for details. The software is very easy to use and takes just a few minutes per day. It costs approximately the same price as a cup of coffee.

You can save even more money by doing it yourself. However, this takes a lot longer and is more labor-intensive. The tips below will help you find what to look for:

9—HOW FULL ARE YOU?

This is an easy question. You may be charging too much if you feel less full than you should at this stage. You may be charging too much if you are more full than you expected.

You can get an idea of how much price changes affect the demand for your hotel by changing your prices frequently. This is called the 'price elasticity of demand' in economics. If you lower prices, you will get more bookings the more flexible your customers.

If you are experiencing difficulties, your 'fair price' is likely to be lower than what you are charging. To make up the lost ground, you'll need to lower your price slightly below the "fair" price. You'll need to sell more rooms in the remaining time.

You are losing money if you have empty rooms that could have been sold at a lower rate than what you were charging.

You are also losing money if you sell your rooms for less than the market value. While guests may be happy if you charge less than fair, it is actually a way of making them happy. You would rather your guests were happy because they received good service, than because you gave them a figurative envelope with PS20?

10—BUT DON'T BE TOO EXPENSIVE

It might be possible to charge three times the normal rate for hotel rooms in busy times and still have enough room, but it might not be a good idea.

Hotels can change their prices within a certain range of comfort. They expect it to be a routine. People expect to pay more for Center Parcs during school holidays than they do in term time. People get upset when you go beyond that range. It could be argued that this violates their notion of fairness from a behavioural economics perspective.

You can get away with this if you're a Cardiff hotel and the Champions League Final takes place at your local stadium. Guests won't be returning to your hotel anyway. Customers often see this behavior as price gouging and will seek to correct it in the future.

In addition, although customers may pay a lot for a room their idea of value is dependent on the price paid. If they pay clearly too much, then their satisfaction and (equally importantly) review score will be lower. You need to avoid having your guests feel that they got bad value.

Assuming you have a high-volume repeat business, I would suggest setting the maximum price at 50% above your average price. If your business is event-driven and not loyalty-based, you can increase it.

11—AND DON'T BE TOO CHEAP EITHER

If your rooms are not being used, it may be tempting to offer them for a very low price to help you fill them up. This is a good idea for a short-term. It costs PS10 per room for variable costs, and 10 rooms can be sold for PS40. That's PS300 that you have made back from your fixed costs.

This is not a long-term solution for two reasons.

It makes your rooms look too expensive and gives people a negative impression of your hotel. This makes it look like a low-end hotel, so people will place it in that category. It may not get as many bookings as you expect. It lowers future price expectations. It will be difficult to convince clients to pay PS150 again if you charge them PS150 for the same room they paid PS40.

There are two exceptions to this rule: 1) If you can sell them via a blind platform such as Priceline. Customers get a better deal if they don't know which hotel they will be getting. You can also sell them to tour operators where the price is hidden in the package. These methods don't lower the brand or reduce future price expectations, argue I.

You may attract guests that Basil Fawlty would not approve of if your prices are too low!

To sum it all, I recommend setting a minimum price of 60% for your average hotel price in order to prevent any long-term damage to your hotel's reputation.

12—STRIKE-THROUGH PRICING

OTAs agree that strikes through pricing is a way to drive bookings. This is where the original price of a product or service is removed and replaced with a lower price. How can you convince them to display your pricing as strike-through pricing? Your prices should be different on different days. OTAs typically take the most expensive price for a given period of time around travel dates. They then subtract that number. The more you discount on the highest price day, the greater the discount. Variable pricing has a hidden advantage. It isn't a discount but it appears like one.

13—MOVE PRICES DOWN AS BOOKING DATE GETS CLOSER

Do you know that rooms prices can be reduced by 10-15% in the days leading up to guest arrivals? Although this is an average, it does not always hold. However, hotels with availability will try to lure late-booking guests to choose their hotel. There is a good chance that Mr. Late Booker will choose a competitor if you don't lower your prices.

14--A LOOK AT WHAT HOTELS CHARGING IN THE NEIGHBOURHOOD

Your nearest rivals are the hotels in your neighborhood. They are directly in competition with you. They will be more popular if they offer better perceived value than yours. You will attract more people if you offer better perceived value. If you feel full, you can offer less value (lower prices) while still attracting enough people. You will have to be more valuable if you feel empty.

***15--LOOK AT THE CHARGE OF LARGE HOTELS IN VICINITY** Remember that revenue managers are full-time employees of large hotels. They are responsible for predicting future demand. They will know if there are concerts in the area. They will be the first to know if there's a sunny weekend. They have more space to sell so they know ahead of time if there will be quiet. You can benefit from their work and access their data by looking at their prices.*

16—SHOULDER NIGHTS AND GROUP BOOKINGS

Let's say you have a full schedule on Saturday, but are not busy on Friday and Sunday. How likely are you to get full on Friday? Reasonable low, unless your prices are reduced, as many guests would rather stay on Friday or Saturday than go somewhere else. In this instance, Friday and Sunday are known as shoulder nights. The head is Saturday when you feel full. These "shoulder nights" are difficult to sell and can result in large income losses. You need a strategy.

Is it a good idea to book a group booking that takes up more than half of your hotel room for one night? It all depends on how busy you are. But remember, if you're full, you block off other customers who might have booked for more than one night. Before you make a decision, I recommend thinking carefully.

I wouldn't offer free cancellations. You will not have any guests if they cancel.

There are two good ways to deal shoulder night-related issues. I recommend that you use both. The first is price. You should charge more Saturday than Friday if Saturday is more popular than Friday. This discourages bookers from booking Saturday nights, and encourages them to book Friday only. Bookers who book both Saturday and Friday nights may lose on Saturday, but make a profit on Friday. This could lead to them breaking even.

This means you'll get more Friday night bookings than your competitors and fewer Saturday nights bookings.

Another way to address this issue is to establish a minimum stay requirement, such as a 2-night minimum.

17—WHEN TO USE MINIMUM STAY REQUIREMENTS

In most cases, using price is more advantageous than using minimum stays. Because you can get guests who are looking to stay for 2 nights or less, as well as those who are interested in staying one night, this is a good idea. This means you have more customers and can charge slightly more.

But, this may not be the case in all cases.

Imagine that Saturday night is the big event. All hotels in the city will be booked. It is possible to charge five times the normal rate and still have full rooms. This is possible if you have customers who aren't likely to return. If you don't want to charge so much, there are other ways to get the most out of the situation.

For nights where the 'fair price' - the price at which you would make the most money overall - is higher that the price you wish to charge, minimum stay requirements can be very helpful. What should you do if you can charge PS200, but don't want the price to exceed PS150? That's it. This will reduce demand and increase income, but not exceed your maximum price of PS150.

18—HOW TO USE FREE CANCELLATION

Customers love free cancellation. Why shouldn't they? They don't know what the future holds and don't want to pay a large hotel bill if they change their minds. Customers will pay more for hotels that offer free cancellation.

Customers, especially business customers, are willing to cancel their bookings for free in the event that they are not there. They can cancel at any time, and it reserves a place for them.

Customers who see that the price has dropped since their original booking will be able to cancel and book again.

How can a hotel owner handle all this?

The important thing is to remember that cancellations are free if you cancel.

a) Your hotel was not going to be full anywayYou can sell the room that was cancelled.The only thing that will cost you is if you cancel too soon to make a new booking. In times when you are not working, you can offer cancellations free of charge (charging a few percent more).

You should examine the impact of busy times on your business. Are you getting a lot businesspeople calling and cancelling when you are full? Are you worse off if they cancel? Don't offer cancellations free of charge during busy seasons, if so. This should be left to larger hotels that can book - as we will discuss in the next tip.

By the way, if you go to roompricegenie.com/freecancellationcalculator you can try various calculations to determine how much you should charge on top of your normal price.

19—CAN YOU USE OVERBOOKING?

You know that between 5-10% of your cancellations will be cancelled as a hotel manager. This is dependent on the hotel. These bookings could be covered if you had 5-10% more availability.

You can do this if you have a large hotel with 100 bedrooms. Your estimate will be accurate due to the law of large numbers. You can take the guest to a better hotel if you're lucky (about twice per year). You can inform them that the bathroom is not working properly (this happened once to us - I'm not sure if it was actually a problem).

It is very difficult for a small hotel to do this, unless they have a high cancellation rate (in that case I would suggest stopping offering free cancellation). If you have 20 rooms and a 10% cancellation policy, then two rooms on average will be empty. There is still a 13% chance everyone will show up. If you overbook 1 room per night, you'll have to move one guest to another hotel about once a week.

It may be worth it for 6 additional bookings for other nights. It doesn't offer great service to customers.

20—UPGRADES

Let's say you have two types of rooms - expensive and cheap. The cheapest rooms cost PS80 while the most expensive are PS110. Imagine that all the rooms in your budget are gone and you still have three of your more expensive rooms.

Two people could be upgraded to your expensive rooms by upgrading their rooms. You will then have two rooms that are cheap and one room that is expensive. In this situation, you are more likely get a full-booked hotel.

You can offer availability to both luxury-oriented customers and guests who are more sensitive to price. Your potential clients will be more interested in your cheaper rooms if they are available.

You can also make someone who had booked a room at a lower price and is now upgraded into a happier customer.

Who should you upgrade? We will investigate this further, but it is generally to reward clients who have given you more money and to incentivise future clients.

Recurrent clients are the first to upgrade. These are people who have been to your area many times and deserve to be treated like royalty.

You should then upgrade those who booked directly through you. Your website should clearly state that upgrades are given preference to direct bookers. This will encourage people to book via your website. This extra value is free and will give them an incentive to book next time.

21—ROOM PRICE GENIE SOFTWARE

Without a plug for our software, this section wouldn't be complete. With roompricegenie.com, most of the above mentioned can be accomplished with minimal effort at a low cost. You can get a free 1-month trial or a double guarantee. We guarantee that if you're not satisfied within 6 months, we will refund all fees paid and send you a box chocolates. It will transform your company, we are so confident. Tip number 21:

Register now at roompricegenie.com to get a free trial.

SELLING ON VALUE NOT PRICE

As we have already mentioned, pricing is important. Pricing is only one aspect. Customers are more likely to book if they perceive more value. This is the trick: Give them value that doesn't cost you much.

Customers should love the hotel's value so much they don't care about its cost.

This will be covered in detail later, in the section about customer reviews. Hotels are evaluated based on the value they received and the price they paid. Many of these factors can help improve perceived value.

This section is short and contains two tips. This section focuses on giving extra value and making sure that guests are aware of the additional value before they book.

22—GIVE MORE VALUE

Do a brainstorming session with your staff/partner/friends. You can think of ways you can provide more value to your customers for a lower cost.

Superlative service is a clear way to do it. A hotel's perception will change dramatically if they offer friendly, helpful service. You should take them to their rooms if you are able. You can show them the facilities, discuss local activities with them, and even recommend restaurants. It doesn't matter if there is a strange smell or the toilet flushes, the guest will not be able to criticize hosts who are so kind.

It is possible that there are many walkers who visit your hotel. You can offer expert advice about the local walks with maps and local knowledge. Other ways you can offer more are also possible. What is the cost of a welcome drink? It will be a great welcome drink after a long journey.

Would you be willing to offer tea and coffee for free? These items are not expensive but guests will be very grateful.

23—TELL THEM ABOUT YOUR EXTRA VALUE

You can mention that you offer walking guidance if you have a hotel. We offer maps and tips."

Offer tea and coffee for free? Tell them, "Unlimited free teas or coffees included in the pricing"

You might have very nice beds, so make sure to check out your reviews.

Communicating the benefits is important as they will increase the perceived value and make your guests happier to pay more.

You can read reviews to find out what guests love about the hotel.

Even after all this, it is important to keep a few value-adds secret, such as a welcome beverage. These positive surprises can help improve your review scores. This brings us to...

CUSTOMER REVIEWS

The importance of reviews and scores has been a major change in the hotel industry over the last 15 years. This has made it easier for guests to review hotels and forced them to improve their service. A hotel that offers customer service like Basil Fawlty's would be forced to close down soon. A small, friendly, well-run hotel can still be expected to earn a fair amount of business.

This section is all about customer reviews, but it could also be placed in the section above that focuses on adding value or the section below that focuses on getting repeat customers. These things are more than a review issue.

Reviews are vital! A 1-point increase in customer reviews (e.g. Hotels can charge 10% more for their rooms if they have a higher customer review score (e.g., from 3 to 4 of 5). They also get half the bookings as before. Your bookings will increase if you improve your rating.

Research has also shown that reviews' content is more important than their average score. People love to hear from guests who are like them. Booking decisions are influenced by the quality of descriptive reviews. Your ranking is determined by reviews over the past year and a quarter. This means that you can do more than what you did in the past. To get more reviews and to increase revenue, you can work on the points mentioned here.

Asking for good reviews is the first step to getting them. Trip Advisor rated Lancaster's second-best restaurant. I went with my friends. To get there, we even made a detour. It was terrible. We were served frozen scampi with horrible humus and mediocre main dishes. There was however a small dish at the table that had Trip Advisor cards inside, which asked for reviews.

It seems that people who are friendly towards the restaurant will be more inclined to leave positive reviews and help others. This would not encourage people to leave negative reviews any more than they were already. Review cards don't make them more vindictive. It worked out for them. We had a horrible meal, but didn't leave any negative reviews. The cards are still the number one in Lancaster.

You should ask for reviews. Ask people who are leaving to rate their stay. They might be willing to rate their experience. Give them a card.

To continue writing negative reviews, you must be determined. You will soon find people writing positive reviews about your hotel.

Politely asking for reviews will increase your review score.

25—REAL-TIME CUSTOMER SATISFACTION SURVEYS

Resolving guest issues before they leave is another important aspect of getting positive reviews. If not possible, at least listen and sympathize with them.

Imagine that a hotel's bathroom has a strange odor. The guest will write a review and say that the bathroom was a problem. This is exactly what you would expect, and it is entirely reasonable from their perspective.

However, let's say you speak to the guest and ask them about their bedroom. Imagine pushing them to ask if they have any suggestions.

You might respond, "Yes, it does, but the bathroom has a strange smell." You could then do one of the following. You could also offer to move the room if you have another room. This will help you solve the problem and almost certainly won't get penalized. Your helpfulness might even lead to you being promoted.

Even if there was no space, you could still acknowledge their problem.

"Yes, there is a problem. The council are working on it and we hope that when they finish, it will be solved. We are all too full, so I would love to change your bedroom. As an apology, I'd like to offer you a drink.

Are they going to give you a negative review if you write it? Most likely not.

You should make it a point to address any issues that guests may have while they're there. Ask them about their satisfaction with their room. Ask them about the location and other factors that are beyond your control. Even though there is nothing you can do, hearing your complaint will help take the pain out of it and make it less likely that they submit it for review.

26--YOUR TAFF SHOULD BE THE FRIENDLIEST & MOST HELPFUL PERSON IN THE AREA

It costs nothing to be friendly. Kind and helpful staff are what make a hotel experience more enjoyable. Training sessions are held regularly in high-quality hotels to remind staff about the standard of service they should expect. Even smaller hotels may be able to do the same thing on a more informal basis. To ensure that certain standards are met, policies should be in place.

I asked one of the hotel owners, whose staff was not very friendly, if he considered friendliness important. He said yes. It is very important. How does he ensure clients get friendly service? He hires for friendliness. However, they didn't seem to be friendly when I interviewed them.

To ensure good service, policies are necessary. This policy can be for you or your staff. This policy states that "we will ask each guest about it". "We will tell each guest about that." "We will give each guest the other." It is possible to create a checklist for each client, and have staff tick off what they have done.

27—OFFER LITTLE EXTRAS

Marketing is based on the notion that customer satisfaction equals perceived performance minus expectations. The customer will be happier if you exceed what they expect. It's a good idea not to reveal too many things. Your superhelpful service will be one. One could be a welcome drink. You could also give them biscuits as a gift for the return journey.

Research has shown that the memories that are most memorable are those that occur at the beginning and end of a trip. Enhancing one of these experiences can help improve their disposition towards you and possibly lead to a higher review score. These things aren't expensive but they are thoughtful.

Similar to the previous theme, a hotel owner told me that surprise meals are a common practice for staff who have done well in recent times. These are great for staff retention and morale, he says. Surprises are good for everyone.

28—KEEP DETAILED NOTES ON CLIENTS

Property management software will let you take notes about each client and their trips. You can use it for this.

It means that a returning customer calls to say "Welcome back Mr Smith, it's great to see you again!" It is a way of remembering the room he was in last time, and that he has a preference for extra pillows. "We have placed you in room 15, which is slightly larger than the 8 you stayed in last year and offers a better view. We have an extra pillow for you. Do you want a wake-up call.

Imagine the feeling you would have as a return guest when you are treated like this. You won't go anywhere else.

You can go even further. If he wishes, you could offer suggestions on what to do next time.

You need to be cautious when you say "I noticed you're with another woman than last time you came".

When you speak to them, use their names and refer back to things they have told you. If she said that she was going to Siam Pearl, or if she recommended it, you can say "Good morning Mrs Jones. Did you sleep well?".

Personal service and attention to detail go a long ways in achieving your goals. Even if you don't have a world-champion memory it is important to keep good notes.

29—SMALL GIFTS IF YOU MAKE A MISTAKE

You must show concern if something happens, whether it is beyond your control or due to an error. If the problem is small, such as a long wait in a line, I would suggest offering a drink or small gift, like a stick of rock. It's one of those small things that don't cost much, but it leads to goodwill. It shows that you care and it's difficult to get angry at someone who is trying their best and is genuinely sorry.

You could offer 50% off your next stay to make up for the bigger issue, such as noise at night that makes it difficult for them to sleep. You can get them back while showing your care and compassion. These are only suggestions. However, I believe that it is sensible that, if they have a bad experience, you show them that you care and that you are working to improve it.

This helps you get repeat bookings and improves your review score.

YOUR WEBSITE AND OTHER ONLINE SALES CHANNELS

Your website is your public face. Your website should reflect you in the best possible light. You want people to book online. To make sure they book through your website.

People will visit your website from an online travel agency to check if there are better deals or to help you. You want to make sure they book with you when they do.

There are restrictions on what price you can charge online travel agents - you cannot offer a lower price than they do - but you can make it more appealing to visitors to book directly.

Roompricegenie is offering a service that will help you make a website that generates more sales.

For more information on how Roompricegenie.com can assist you, please contact us.

This section contains information on how to sell rooms online, without the use of online travel agencies.

30—USE ANALYTICS

The internet has many advantages in marketing. One is the ability to track customers' behaviours. How would you have known how many sales an advertisement made if it was placed on a billboard in the past? It was impossible. You can now, however. It is possible to see who visited your site, where they came from and what they did once they arrived. It is important to keep records because this will help you determine what works and what does not.

Google Analytics can be used to monitor everything. Install Google Analytics by adding code to each page. This code records where visitors have come from and what they do. This code can be used to create events that you can track, such as clicking on a link or booking.

These are the most important numbers to keep track of:

a.   Number of unique visitors – This is the number of people who have visited your site. Advertising (see below), PR work that gets links from other sites (also seen below), and search engine optimization (also shown below) are all ways to increase your site's visitors. You can track the number of people visiting your site (and be aware of seasonal variations), and use this information to determine how effective your marketing efforts were.Conversion rate is the rate at which people visit your site and convert them into bookers. This is an important metric that you should improve by making your website more conversion-focused. Below are some suggestions.Bookings by Source: How many bookings are you getting from each source? You should improve your search engine performance if you are getting lots of Google searches. You can get more results from specific listings if you want to be more prominently listed in them and in similar listings. It is possible to calculate the cash value of each source so that you can target your promotional time accordingly.31—LARGE PHOTOS, CLEAR DESCRIPTIONS

Just as with your online travel agent profiles, you need to present your hotel in the best possible light. This means high quality, high definition, professionally taken photos. Aim for 30-50 different pictures. Photos of all room types, bathrooms, common areas, garden, breakfast, all amenities, anything that tells the guest what their stay will be like. They should be large and easy to find.

Also, as with the OTA profile, you need to clearly describe all the amenities and benefits offered to guests. Make sure that the visitors know all the wonderful things that they will experience at your hotel. All the things you can do for them. All your strengths should be clearly explained.

32—KEEP IT STANDARD

Some hotel owners fall into the trap of putting too much personality into their website. Your personality is without doubt great. And the people who book through your website may well love what you've done — that's why they booked. But statistics show that, with a few exceptions, keeping everything 'standard' will get you more bookings.

If you think about it, standard appeals to everyone. It doesn't put anyone off. It's just there and you feel like if you stay at this hotel everything will be fine.

Kooky, on the other hand, only appeals to people who are into that particular style of kooky. This limits your clientele base considerably so, although the people who do book will love it, you will get fewer bookings.

Now, if you like running your hotel as an extension of your own personality and don't really mind if it costs money, that's perfectly fine. But bear in mind that those that like your personal style will be likely to tell you and those who don't will be unlikely to do so. If the latter outweigh the former you could be losing business without realizing.

On a similar note, I would try to avoid putting full-wall murals of babies in unusual scenes on the bedroom walls. I say this because some friends showed us photos of one such room recently in quite an expensive hotel in Switzerland, and similarly, although I'm sure some guests loved it, it can be off-putting to others.

I am not saying don't put any individualism into your hotel. It is your hotel and should be an expression of yourself. But maybe you could keep the individualism more on the low-key side.

33—CONVERSION FOCUSED COPY

The copy on your website is all there to get people to book your hotel. As such, it should be fit for purpose. I find a lot of hotel owners are quite understated types. They don't want to show off. In the room descriptions they might say: "the double, while not quite as big as the twin is still a good size and is quite bright as well, although not as bright as the suite".

While they should say: "Our double room is large, bright and airy, with a king-size bed for a perfect night's sleep". That's one I made up — a professional copywriter could do better still.

I would always recommend getting a professional copywriter to look over your website text. It may cost £100, but it is money well spent. In fact, this is so important that it is one of the services we will include for customers of our website builder.

34—BEST PRICE GUARANTEE

In order for your customers to book through your website, they want to be sure that they could not get a better deal elsewhere. This is why you should always state very clearly on your website that you offer a BEST PRICE GUARANTEE. You are basically guaranteeing them that the price will not be cheaper anywhere else.

With the rate parity agreement, you sign with the OTA, you are not allowed to go lower than them, but you can offer the same price (the joint best price) and you could also say that bookings through the website are more likely to get upgrades. You could also offer other incentives like late check-out or a free welcome pack.

Note that sometimes the OTA will (by reducing its own commission) be able to offer your room at a cheaper rate than is stated on your website. If the client finds this, you will need to honour that rate.

35—MOBILE FRIENDLY WEBSITE

According to the latest research 40% of searches and 25% of bookings, on a popular OTA, were executed from mobile devices. And this number is rising.

You need to make sure that your hotel's website looks equally spectacular on a mobile phone screen or tablet as it does on a desktop computer.

It also needs to load quickly as slow load times lead to customers going elsewhere.

Take time to develop your mobile site and don't just see it as an afterthought.

36—VERIFIED USER REVIEWS

People love reviews. Make sure your website has a lot of reviews available to the reader. Make sure that the reviews cover all areas of the hotel. If you have a food page, put reviews of the food on it. On the rooms page put reviews of how well the guests slept. On the location page put quotes about how well located you are. You can, and should, link to the actual reviews for verification.

Also put your Trip Advisor and Booking.com rating on your site using one of their widgets. It builds trust. If potential guests can see the review score there, they don't need to go to Trip Advisor, where they might be tempted by another hotel.

The higher up you are in search engine results, the more people will click on your hotel and the more people will book. If you are a hotel in Sunderland, then you want your hotel to come up first when someone types hotels in Sunderland into Google. Or at least in the top 10.

How do you get yourself higher up what are referred to as the SERPS (search engine result pages)? There are whole books on the subject, and I can't give a detailed list, but I can outline some general principles.

First, the days when you could trick the search engines by writing loads of invisible text using your keywords are long gone. The search engines – and it's Google you need to be primarily concerned with – got wise to that little trick years ago. In fact, they punish you for trying these ruses and move you down their rankings or even kick you out altogether. To succeed in the SERPS now, you need to concentrate on providing a genuine service to the searcher.

How do the little Google bots determine this? Links from other websites are important. If you can contact local directory sites - and anyone you think may link to you - and get them to do so, then this gets you higher, or it should. It also gets you more visitors to your websites from these places so is a good thing to do anyway, as long as you are making the right 'friends'. Links from dubious websites will get your site penalized, so do be careful with advisors promising you search engine riches.

Another important part of SEO – search engine optimisation - is content. If you provide high quality content – photos, videos and blog content, then your SERPS ranking will rise. Use a blog feature to offer value to searchers by describing local venues and restaurants. Give them information. This boosts your search rankings but it also means that people will be more likely to book with you as you are positioning yourself as a helpful source of information.

Speed is increasingly important to Google as well. speed. Make sure your website is tested and optimised to load quickly. This is good for search engine optimisation, but once again also good for business, as a slow loading page leads to people clicking away to other options out of frustration In summary, this tip would be to buy a book on search engine optimisation and make sure that your website is up to standard.

38—___CONTENT___

As described above, you need great content for search engine optimisation.

But more than that, content can be a way to attract new visitors. If someone Googles "walks in the lake district", and you have a blog on walks in the lake district then people will click on your link. When it comes to booking a hotel, there's a reasonable chance they'll choose yours as you have shown yourselves to be experts.

Similarly, "Sights in Bournemouth" could come up with your list of tourist attractions. Once again, when it comes to booking their hotel, you will be well placed in the searcher's mind thanks to your obvious local expertise

In general, the more information, photos and videos your site offers, the more you are providing to the visitor and the better their experience. And from this comes more bookings.

39—PAY PER CLICK

One option you have these days, instead of paying OTAs, is to do your own internet advertising. There are various ways to do this and generally it will work out that you pay for the number of people who click on the link to your website. Once again, there are whole books on this, but it might be something to try out. If you can get bookings for a lower price than it costs on the online travel agents, then you might wish to continue it.

The market leader here is Google with its AdWords offering. Here you put in some key phrases "Hotels in Bournemouth" might be an example, and then every time someone searches for "Hotels in Bournemouth" your hotel will be one of the sponsored results at the top of the page. Depending on how popular the search term is, you will need to pay a varying amount of money to get onto that list. I would always start low and move up in price slowly (I was given opposite advice by the AdWords salesman funnily enough). Every time someone clicks on the link to your website, you owe Google money. But if your cost per booking (total cost divided by total number of bookings) is reasonable it may be a good way to get new business.

There are other offerings. For example, you can get a tracking code that means that every time someone visits your website a 'cookie' is put in the files of the visitor – Facebook Pixel is one example of this. If you put a little bit of code from Facebook on your website, then when your website visitor next goes onto Facebook they'll see an advert for your hotel. This could prompt them into making a booking that they had not yet completed. Once again you pay per click onto your website, as well as a small amount for each view. This is particularly effective advertising as you are only targeting people you know are interested.

40—GOING TO META-SITES DIRECTLY.

There are some sites, such as Trivago and Kayak, that amalgamate all of the available OTAs to give the searcher the best price possible. These are very popular with users because they know they are getting the best rate, but they don't have to do too much grunt work to get it. Other important amalgamation platforms are Trip Advisor, which is trusted for having the most reviews, and Google Hotel Ads which shows your hotel when people are searching on Google maps. Not many hotel owners know that you can also list on these sites directly - saving yourself the commission you pay when you go through the OTAs. The terms and conditions of these sites vary, and can be on a pay per click basis, but often it will end up much better for you than paying the commission.

I would certainly suggest registering on these sites as you have nothing to lose by doing so. Here is a list of some: Trivago: www.trivago.com/hotelmanager/register

Kayak: www.kayak.com/hotelowner

Trip Advisor Instant Booking:
www.tripadvisor.com/TripAdvisorInsights/n2513/faq-instant-bookingtripadvisor

Google Hotel Ads: www.google.com/intl/en/ads/hotels/

41—OTHER SALES CHANNELS

You can also consider other sales channels. There is a very simple rule here; the more people who see your availability, the more bookings you will get. Other ways you can increase the number of potential guests that see your rooms are by selling through tour operators and by using an opaque selling model.

Tour operators used to be the medium through which most people booked their holidays. They were popular for their ease of booking through one place, combined with the personal advice at a time when such information was difficult to come by. Also, when sold as a package a holidaymaker would not be liable to pay for their hotel if their flight were cancelled.

The industry has changed and the proliferation of information over the internet has meant that tour operators tend to operate only in more niche areas. But they still need rooms, and if your rooms are available, then they might book them. Tour operators work through a system called GDS (Global Distribution System) which connects to your property management system via the channel manager. You can look into whether this works for your business by speaking to a GDS provider.

As a word of warning, with all dealings with different channels, you need to make sure that you are working on the 'Retail model' where all rooms can be made available to all channels and you pay for each booking. The other option, the 'Merchant model', means you would guarantee availability to a certain provider who can return the rooms to you at will.

Another way you could sell more rooms is by using an 'opaque model' like Priceline. Priceline is useful if you have a lot of rooms to sell but don't want to make your rooms any cheaper for business reasons. On Priceline, you can offer your rooms at a heavily discounted price, but the guest won't know it's your hotel until they've already booked. In return for not knowing which hotel they are booking, they get a cheaper price. And in return for being able to sell your room without adversely affecting your long-term business, you offer that cheaper price on the opaque platform.

SECTION 4B

OTHER BUSINESS IMPROVEMENTS

The main message from this section is that you are paying a lot of money to the online travel agents to find you clients. It's up to you to make the most of this. As mentioned above, you could view the OTAs as billboards for your business. They are great at giving you exposure places where you never would have had it. The challenge for you is to make sure that you keep the guest as your client. Otherwise some of that expensive OTA fee has been wasted and you've lost a profitable guest in the future.

A lot of this is already covered in the Section 3 on customer reviews. However, there are other tactics that you could use as well, and these are listed below.

There are different tips here too. Upselling and segmentation are both strategies pursued by larger hotels that, to a lesser extent can be used by you as well, in order to increase the value of your clients to you. And utilisation of free publicity is a way to avoid OTA fees in the first place.

42—DISCOUNT CODES FOR REPEAT BOOKERS

Every time a guest stays at your hotel, make sure that you give them a card at the end with a code on it. This code could give them 5% off if they book directly through your hotel website. This is a win-win for everyone involved.

The guest knows that they are getting a special deal and feels rewarded for loyalty. They pay less and so are happier with the service.

At the same time, you potentially get a booking you wouldn't have otherwise got (as they appreciate the discount), and potentially someone who normally books through an OTA goes directly to your site, saving you most of the commission.

You could also create a membership scheme that allows login on your website. You can offer any loyalty rewards you like behind the login - it is not covered by the rate parity agreements demanded by the OTAs as only public prices are covered.

To repeat this (as it's very important), as a rule you really need to make sure to reward customers who book again because these customers may well be regular visitors and provide you with a lot of business in the future. Do everything you can to keep them happy.

43—OTHER THINGS TO KEEP GUESTS HAPPY

As soon as you have identified someone as a repeat customer - either because they have booked twice or because you know from conversation that they come regularly to the area- you want to treat them with even more care. As previously mentioned, for example, the first people to get upgrades should be repeat customers.

Make sure to tell them about your discount scheme for past guests.

If you have a restaurant, why not offer them a free dessert (especially if they weren't planning on buying one anyway) as they are one of your treasured guests.

You could leave a free bottle of wine in their room on arrival with a handwritten note saying welcome back.

You can use your imagination here, but these little things help build a good feeling about you in a guest's mind and make them more likely to return.

44—KEEP AN EMAIL LIST

To encourage loyalty and keep your hotel in your guests' thoughts, ask for email addresses. Every few months, send them a newsletter with special offers, news from the area such as local festivals, and anything else you think may be of interest to them. Whenever you write a new blog article about local attractions you could send it to your list.

Use an email platform like Mailchimp, which allows readers to easily unsubscribe, as you don't want to spam anyone. But the clients who don't unsubscribe are enjoying the updates and more likely to book at your hotel in future.

45—CHRISTMAS CARDS

Sending an online Christmas card to your email list is free, virtually never unwelcome, and keeps you in their thoughts. There is no reason not to do it really. It is little touches like this that make guests remember you and if they remember you, they are a little more likely to book with you again.

46—UPSELLING

Apart from your rooms, are there any additional, valuable products or services that you provide to your clients, or could provide? With upselling, the idea is that at the time of purchase or on arrival you try to encourage the guest to spend more money at your hotel.

An obvious upselling opportunity is an on-site restaurant. You would really like the guest to stay for dinner, and at the same time it is convenient for the guest to stay for dinner. But sometimes they will go out to eat locally and you will miss out.

What if, when people book, you offer them a special offer on the set menu — that can only be purchased in advance. Since they know they need to eat and know they are getting a good deal, they may very well take you up on this. They will be happy because they got a good price and they won't have to waste precious holiday time arguing about where to eat. You will be happy because you have an extra plate sold at every sitting and also you can plan in advance more easily as you know you have definite restaurant guests.

You could also ask local attractions if they have any arrangements whereby you sell tickets for them so that the guest gets a discount and you get commission. If you have a few of these offers, you're offering a valuable service to your guests by giving them options on where to go and offering discounts to go there. And you're increasing income to yourself.

If you don't have a restaurant you could see if local restaurant can offer the same arrangement, where you send clients to them with a voucher and you get commission.

In all cases here, make sure that what you are doing is providing the customer with a great service, that you happen to be profiting from. Only look for winwin situations. If you are sending them to a bad restaurant or boring attraction they won't thank you for it and you won't have benefited long-term.

47—SEGMENTATION

Segmentation is a complicated subject and it is difficult for small hotel owners to implement, but I will briefly discuss it in case it gives you any ideas.

Segmentation simply means separating your customers into different groups and treating these groups differently.

To understand how larger hotels might use this – think about, for example, casino hotels in Las Vegas. They have data that states that certain customers tend to gamble large amounts of money in their hotel casino when they stay there. They know that if they offer one such client accommodation for $50 a night they will more than make up for the loss of room revenue with expected casino profits. Likewise, someone who spends a lot at the restaurant or on the golf course.

They may also know that some clients are more price sensitive. They can offer deals to those clients that they don't offer to less price-sensitive clients who book anyway. In your case this could be a pensioner's coach tour, who you know won't book unless they're getting the best possible deal.

In some ways you may be already doing some form of segmentation – by treating returning guests to extra value, you are rewarding people whom you hope will give you more business in future. By giving upgrades to those who book directly through your website, you are encouraging people to book in a way that gives you more revenue.

Often the key to effective segmentation is good data. The more data you have on your clients, the better you can use it to their and your advantage. In this sense the larger hotels have the upper hand as they have more clients and better data collection capabilities.

But you too can and should keep track of all information you know about a client on your hotel management system. Knowledge is power, as the old saying goes.

48—ASSOCIATION WITH NEARBY CLUBS, BUSINESSES, ETC.

What is it that attracts people to your area? What are the guests doing when they arrive? Talk to your guests to find the purpose of their visit.

Then think of ways you can make an arrangement with any organisations involved.

If people are coming on business trips, what is their business? Does their company send other people here? If so, you could ask the guest who is the person in their company who organises the trips. You can then call them directly and offer 10% off for any direct bookings with you. Try to keep up good relations with that business manager, and you could become the default hotel in your area for that business.

Maybe they are coming for a chess tournament in the area. In that case, get in touch with the organisers of the chess tournament and ask to be featured on their website. You could offer them commission if anyone books through you.

Maybe your guests are mountaineers. If so, go to the local mountaineering association and ask to be featured on their website – you could offer all members of that club a special welcome pack with handwarmers and a packed lunch.

Whatever the reason may be, this is your opportunity to get more bookings for your hotel and usually at lower commission rates than the online travel agents are charging.

Don't let these opportunities just pass you by.

49—HAVE THE RIGHT ATTITUDE AND GET THE RIGHT ADVICE

In the end, there are two things needed to improve your business. One is the right attitude. You need a mind open to improvement combined with a commitment to implement new things. Some changes you try will work and some won't, but if you don't try you'll never know some of them might have been a great success. And I guarantee that if you try enough things, some will be a great success. You need to be able to accept criticism from guests and see how it can help you make your service better. If you have an attitude of always improving where you can, the sky is the limit.

The second necessary factor is good advice. There are a lot of suggestions here, and if you are interested you can look further into these. There are many books available with more specific information and I recommend reading and learning. We are all learning all the time – or we should be - and there are a lot of experts out there who can help.

On that note, if you were to decide to sign up with Roompricegenie.com, we do not just promise to increase your revenue using our advanced pricing technology. We consider that we are in a partnership with you, and looking to improve your business in every way. As a member, if you have any questions feel free to ask and hopefully we can either help or guide you in the right direction to someone who can.

Equally, as part of the partnership, we would hope that you would tell us if you see us doing things wrong, so that we can improve our business too.